TESTIMONIALS

Since I came in contact with Mr. Ekwueme in 2010, I discovered that he is a man of integrity with the Love of God in him. He is an active member of the youth group at Winner's Chapel International, Connecticut. He distinguished himself as a dependable and reliable member of the church. I love to be around him. Ike Ekwueme is a social person who has the ability to relate with any group of people. He is a man of honor.

—Kolawole Adebayo, Pastor
Winner's Chapel International, Connecticut

Ike Ekwueme is a deep thinker, an engaging writer, and an exceptional person. He combines intelligence with grace, and his positive outlook on life will no doubt touch all those who read his words of wisdom. In my 23 years of teaching college students, I have met few people with Ike's sunny disposition and thirst for knowledge.

—Bruce Johnson, Professor,
American International College, United States

Ike is a born leader with a unique passion for success. He is filled with positive energy, an abundance of intelligent ideas, and he brings a spark of creativity, which puts him a step ahead of the rest. Working alongside Ike was certainly a privilege, as he set a great example for all teammates, classmates, and audiences.

—Lauren Phillips, Student,
American International College, United States

SWITCH ON
AND
STAND OUT

SWITCH ON AND STAND OUT

Unless otherwise stated, all scriptures are from the New Living Translation Bible.

Library of Congress Control Number: 2015939302

ISBN: 978-1-63308-134-5 Print
         978-1-63308-135-2 Digital

Interior and Cover Design by R'tor John D. Maghuyop

1028 S Bishop Avenue, Dept. 178
Rolla, MO 65401

Printed in United States of America

SWITCH ON
— AND —
STAND OUT

17 Spiritual Truths
that Transformed
My Life

IKE EKWUEME

CHALFANT ECKERT
PUBLISHING

TABLE OF CONTENTS

ACKNOWLEDGEMENTS

First of all, I thank God for giving me the inspiration and determination to write this book. Also, I want to express my gratitude to my immediate family: my parents, brothers, and sister for their continuous support of my goals and dreams, and my extended family for their encouragement. My church families have been an integral part of my Christian development and include Winners Chapel International, King's Church Manchester, and the Overseas Fellowship of Nigerian Christians (OFNC). It is through these Christian ministries that I was nurtured to become the person I am today. Also, I want to thank all my mentors, supporters and well-wishers: God Bless you all.

ABOUT THE BOOK

Until age 18, I struggled with lack of identity and motivation. I was neither up nor down. I was living someone else's life; I was not myself. Anytime I looked in the mirror, it was almost like I was seeing someone else's face. I was afraid to express the whole essence of who I was. I am grateful for all the advice I received growing up and I am thankful for all the experiences that God allowed me to go through. I wrote this book as an expression of who I am. I made a decision to be myself and be my best. I'm working at it every day.

My approach to life and my thinking has been transformed by spiritual truths. In this book, I explain some of the spiritual truths that I have learned so far in life. I share these truths using different styles of writing. I included poems, short stories, biblical scriptures, quotes, dialogues, and personal testimonies to give you a better understanding and an interesting reading experience. All the poems in this book were inspired by God and written by me. Although this book was written by me, it is also for me. I strive to practice what I preach every day.

As you switch on the principles in this book, I believe that you will stand out and be outstanding in your life. God Bless you as you read along.

INTRODUCTION

Bob: Hello, I'm Bob. What's your name?

Ike: Ike (EE-KAY)

Bob: What does E.K. stand for?

Ike: Actually, my full name is Chukwubuikem Ekwueme. I was born in Nigeria.

Bob: And you're not ashamed to say it. Some people would have changed their names.

Ike: You're right. But let me tell you a lesson I learned about identity…

IDENTIFY WITH YOUR IDENTITY

· · · · · · · · · · ◉ · · · · · · · · · · ·

We all came from somewhere; identify with that somewhere.
When someone asks you: "Where are you from?"-Don't say
elsewhere.
I lived in Europe, but my name says Nigeria;
That's my birthplace and I came from her.

My roots have contributed to who I am;
I still eat plantain and pounded yam-
I've not lost my identity, I am what I am:
My name is Chukwubuikem, not Adam.

· · · · · · · · · · ◉ · · · · · · · · · · ·

But you may ask, "Why are you called Ike?"
Let's take attendance and find out.

Attendance

Professor: James
James: Yes, ma'am.
Professor: Peter
Peter: Yes, ma'am.

Professor: Mary
Mary: Yes, ma'am.
Professor: Alex
Alex: Yes, ma'am.
Professor: Umm…Chuck a b…
Ike: That's me! 'Chukwubuikem' (Chook-woo-bee-kem).
Ike: But you can call me Ike.

I am from the Igbo tribe. It is common for some names (especially for males) to have 'Ike' in them (pronounced EE-KAY).

Some examples: **Ike**nna, **Ike**chi, **Ike**chukwu, Chukwub**Ike**m. Most of the people who have these names are called 'Ike' as a short form of their full names (American pronunciation "Ay-k", Native pronunciation "EE-KAY").

Embrace Your Uniqueness.

I used to wonder why my parents gave me such a long name. Also, my mother would always give the school my full first name-the full 'Chukwubuikem'. In some cases, the whole name wouldn't fit on the line. Since I started school in England, even if I didn't want attention, my name would direct all attention to me while the teacher took the attendance. In high school, every time we had a new teacher, I had to meet them before the class started so I could tell them to call me 'Ike'. Otherwise, it was guaranteed that someone would laugh while the teacher struggled to pronounce my name. I used to be so embarrassed. One day, during a time of reflection, I said to myself, "Chukwubuikem, you are unique; you are different. Be happy with yourself. Embrace your uniqueness." Now I say my name, anywhere and anytime. To my surprise, many of my friends now call me Chukwubuikem. It rolls off their tongue nicely. It's not as difficult as it looks. Give it a try. Chook-woo-bee-kem.

Chukwubuikem means *God is my Strength*. My name has been my testimony. God has truly been my strength and my helper.

> *I look up to the mountains; does my strength come
> from mountains? No, my strength comes from God,
> who made heaven, and earth, and mountains.*
> Psalm 121: 1-2, (Message Bible)

> *Thank you for making me so wonderfully complex!
> Your workmanship is marvelous—how well I know it.*
> Psalm 139:14,

> *...for I am fearfully and wonderfully made...*
> Psalm 139:14, (King James Version)

> **"When you discover who you are, you will
> be free from everyone else's opinion."**
> (Dr. Myles Munroe)

> **"To be yourself in a world that is constantly
> trying to make you something else is
> the greatest accomplishment."**
> (Ralph Waldo Emerson).

HEART TO HEART

Bob: You were born in Nigeria, you lived in England, and you studied in America…pretty interesting.

Bob: Is there anything else you would like to tell the world?

Ike: Hmmm…

Bob: Speak now or forever hold your peace.

Ike: I'm a Christian and I go to church.

Bob: Church? Why do you go?

Ike: Quick question for you first. Do you have a car?

Bob: Yes.

Ike: What do you do when your fuel goes down?

Bob: Go to the gas station to fill up.

Ike: My life is like your car and church is my gas station.

Bob: Hmm…more explanation please…

Ike: However, I don't wait to be depressed before I go to church, any opportunity I get, I go to top up.

Bob: …Because you keep topping up, you will never be afraid of tomorrow's journey, because you are loaded and ready to overcome the challenges ahead.

Ike: You've got it. That's why I have to be in church.

CHURCH: THE GAS STATION

Church starts at 10:00 a.m.-
Get up bright and early;
It may last a little longer than 12:00 p.m.
But don't leave early.

You may be crying before
But in Church you can't weep;
With the lively music and joy all around
It's impossible to sleep.

You may drag your feet to the door-
It's been a long, hard day;
Just enter, give it five minutes-
You'll definitely want to stay.

There's a lot more to receive;
Just have faith and believe
There is something about Church
I don't want to leave.

I grew up in a Christian family but I wanted to know God for myself. After a long season of ins and outs, wanting to enjoy the pleasures of sin and the pleasures of God, I discovered that I can't serve two masters. I either stick to God fully or stick to the world fully. I chose God and I gave my life to Christ and my life has never been the same. I developed a personal relationship with God. No one needed to force me to church. I knew that was where I needed to be so I could stay on fire for God. To me, church is not optional, it is necessary.

Any time I went into Church, I came out a different man. Church is like my gas station. I believe that it is necessary for me to go there to refuel at least once every week. If I am not able to go to church at a physical location, I connect online. Starting the week without church is not a good start for me.

Every time I step in the church, I feel energized. When I was feeling weak, I said, "if only I could get to church".

It's a Family

While studying at American International College, I went to a church in Hartford, Connecticut called Winners Chapel International. A steady drive to the church would take about 40 minutes, but it was worth the trip.

As an international student in America, my church family was my first group of friends. It was truly a home away from home. I felt a sense of true love coming from the church members. On many occasions, a member from the church would drive to my dorm room to pick me up. At my academic graduation ceremony, many members from the church came to celebrate with me. To my surprise, we had a mini-party afterwards; people brought food and drinks. They made that day special for me and I am truly grateful.

Church is Addictive

During my third year in college, I had a roommate who loved God like I did. We went to Church together. We loved God's presence so much that on some occasions, we went to two different churches on Sunday. We went to Winners Chapel International in Connecticut from 10 a.m. until 12 p.m. Then, we came back to the room to freshen up before going to another local church from 2 p.m. until 4 p.m. Our love for God was driving us. If we didn't have homework or upcoming exams, we would have probably gone to three churches on Sunday!

When you love someone, you get excited when you are going to their house. In the same way, my deep-rooted love for God drives me to church (God's house) on Wednesday and Sunday.

> *I was glad when they said to me, "Let us go to the house of the Lord."*
> Psalm 122:1

The Good Restaurant

You'll agree with me that when you go to a good restaurant, you tell your friends about your experience. I was getting some good spiritual food (the Word of God) at this spiritual restaurant (the church), and I wanted to tell everyone about my favorite restaurant. I knew what I was gaining in church and I wanted everyone around me to come and be blessed as well.

**In church, you don't just get 'food';
you are taught how to cook for yourself.**

**Church doesn't give you an artificial high. It
is a place where you are taught practical steps
to overcome the challenges in your life.**

Church is not a place that pushes you down. "You sinner!" Church is a place that pulls you up. "There is a way out!"

"Most people already know what they're doing wrong. When I get them to church, I want to tell them that you can change." (Joel Osteen)

The Inspiration Center

Jim: Hello, Ben. I would like you to work this Sunday.

Ben: Sir, with all due respect, I won't be available for work because I have church this Sunday.

Jim: This is the third time you have refused to work on Sunday! I didn't want to do this, but…you're going to have to choose.

Ben: Between what, sir?

Jim: Church or work.

Ben: I choose Church sir.

Jim: Why are you so bold to say that?

Ben: Sir, it is the blessings from God that make me successful at my job.

Jim: Go on…

Ben: The idea for the new application I developed came during a church service. While the pastor was preaching, I received inspiration. The company logo I designed that has made us a unique brand was designed in Church. While I was worshipping God, the idea came suddenly.

Jim: Okay. So, church is your place of inspiration?

Ben: Yes, sir. It is what I am taught in church that renews my mind. If you stop me from going to church, you will see how useless I am. Sir, can I ask you a question?

Jim: Yes.

Ben: Do you like me as a person?

Jim: Yes. You're honest, humble, and a true gentleman.

Ben: Well, I wasn't always like this…if you stop me from going to church, you may see my bad side.

Jim: You've convinced me. Please, keep going to church! I don't need any more bad people in this company.

Do you have to go?

Thomas: Hey David, where are you going?

David: To church.

Thomas: Why do you always go to church? You can pray and read your bible at home.

David: Answer this first: Why do you always go to the club? You can sing and dance in your bedroom.

Thomas: I go to hang out with friends and I can dance longer, especially when I see other people dancing.

David: Me, too. I have friends in church and I can pray longer, especially when I see other people praying. If I tried to pray on my own at home, I might fall asleep after 10 minutes.

HEART TO HEART

Ike: Would you like to come to church on Sunday?

Bob: Yes, I will come.

Ike: Great. The church bus will pick you up.

Bob: Did you say you're an usher in church?

Ike: Yes.

Bob: Does the church pay you and all those people who sing in the choir?

Ike: No. We are willing volunteers, who love to serve and God blesses us. We have the heart of a servant.

SERVANT HEART

Service is my desire:
Clothed with humility,
Sweeping the floor in a three-piece suit-
It's not a pity.

To see you happy
Makes my heart merry;
To serve is a privilege-
Payment is not necessary.

I am not working for you;
I don't want compensation.
I only want to serve;
I don't need public adoration.

Whether the world sees me or it doesn't,
A servant doesn't need to boast.
I may come early in the morning, but no one needs to know.
Servants work in secret, without making a show.

The first to come
And the last to leave-
A servant may be rich,
Yet he rolls up his sleeves.

I am privileged to go to a church that has locations around the world. I had the pleasure of visiting the following Winners Chapel Churches:

- Winners Chapel, Connecticut, USA
- Winners Chapel, Massachusetts, USA
- Winners Chapel, Hempstead, New York, USA
- Winners Chapel, Maryland, USA
- Winners Chapel, London, UK
- Winners Chapel, Manchester, UK
- Winners Chapel, Dublin, Ireland
- Winners Chapel, Kubwa, Nigeria
- Winners Chapel, Kaduna, Nigeria
- Winners Chapel, Goshen-Abuja, Nigeria
- Winners Chapel, Canaan Land, Nigeria (Headquarters)

I am grateful to God for the privilege to serve Him. When I arrived in most of these churches, even though it was my first time, I would ask, "Where can I serve?" Nobody needed to force me to serve God. I don't feel comfortable coming to church and sitting idle. I am willing and ready to serve anywhere. By the special grace of God, I have been given the opportunity to stand in the usher's department, drum in the choir, and clean in the sanctuary keeper's department. To my greatest surprise, on some occasions, I was asked to lead a prayer session at a prayer meeting.

What motivates me to serve?

1. My Love for God.

One way to prove my Love for God is to serve him.

>[15] *After breakfast Jesus asked Simon Peter, "Simon son of John, do you love me more than these?"*
> *"Yes, Lord," Peter replied, "you know I love you."*
> *"Then feed my lambs," Jesus told him.*

> *[16] Jesus repeated the question: "Simon son of John, do you love me?"*
> *"Yes, Lord," Peter said, "you know I love you."*
> *"Then take care of my sheep," Jesus said.*
> *[17] A third time he asked him, "Simon son of John, do you love me?"*
> *Peter was hurt that Jesus asked the question a third time. He said,*
> *"Lord, you know everything. You know that I love you."*
> *Jesus said, "Then feed my sheep."*

John 21:15-17

Love is not in word only, but in action. I made it a duty to serve God from my heart.

> *Love God, your God, with your whole heart: love him*
> *with all that's in you; love him with all you've got.*

Deuteronomy 6:5 (The Message)

2. There are blessings for serving God.

God is not wicked. We are not serving Him in vain. Genuine servants are setting themselves up for an abundant, peaceful and healthy life.

> *... Serve only the Lord your God. If you do, I will bless*
> *you with food and water, and I will protect you from*
> *illness. There will be no miscarriages or infertility*
> *in your land, and I will give you long, full lives.*

Exodus 23: 25-26

In 22 years of being on earth, I can boldly say that I am a beneficiary of the blessings of God. There are some things I didn't pray for; God just added them to me. I realize that this is part of my blessing package for serving God. I received a scholarship to study and play soccer in America. I graduated without student debt. I can't remember missing one class because of illness. I graduated with straight A's. During my time as a student in America, I have never lacked any good thing. God supernaturally supplies all my needs, therefore confirming His word again and again. I was physically, academically, spiritually, mentally, financially, and socially well. Dare to believe and serve God with your heart, you will be amazed at what can happen.

> *Seek the Kingdom of God above all else, and live righteously, and he will give you everything you need.*
> Matthew 6:33

> *And my God will supply all your needs according to His riches in glory in Christ Jesus.*
> Philippians 4: 19 (New American Standard Bible)

HEART TO HEART

Bob: I heard some people say that you don't like following the crowd.

Ike: You're right. I don't like doing things simply because everyone is doing it.

Bob: Why?

Ike: The crowd is not always right.

THE CROWD IS NOT ALWAYS RIGHT.

The crowd goes east;
Your experience says west-
Ask God first:
He knows what's best.

The way may look appealing:
Yes, this path leads to wealth;
Beware of that road-
The end may be death.

"There is a way that seems right to a person,
but its end is the way that leads to death"
Proverbs 14:12 (New English Translation Bible)

Hands up

I learned to not follow the crowd from a young age. In elementary school, the teacher asked, "How many of you think Graph A is the correct answer?" It seemed like everyone in the class put their hand up, but I didn't. I didn't know why it was the wrong answer; I just knew it was wrong. Something inside me told me. Then, the teacher asked, "How many of you think Graph B is the correct answer?" I was the only person with my hand up. The teacher said I was correct. This experience taught me a significant lesson: Even if a million people are going one way, it doesn't make it the right way. Anytime I find myself tempted to follow the crowd and do something that is wrong, I remind myself of this experience. Don't make assumptions; ask God, and He will guide you on the path that is best for you. Just because everyone is doing it doesn't make it right.

Lone soldier

In one of my courses in college, the professor gave us the opportunity to take the final exam earlier than the actual date if we wanted to. Most people in the class chose to do it early. However, I was not ready. I needed to study more. I chose the later date. I didn't let the fact that everyone was taking the exam early move me to take it early. When I took the exam, I was the only person in the classroom. Everyone else wanted to start their summer holidays early. I prepared effectively for the exam and I got an A grade. If I followed the crowd and I failed the exam, who should I blame? Me. There will always be groups around us whose decisions may push or pull us in one direction or the other. At those sensitive moments, we have to stop, think, listen to the Spirit, and do what is best for ourselves.

Your own ears will hear him. Right
behind you a voice will say,
"This is the way you should go,"
whether to the right or to the left.
Isaiah 30:21

We have to pay attention to that still, small voice.

HEART TO HEART

Bob: I am glad you mentioned that. Some time ago, I wanted to go somewhere, but something inside me told me not to go. It was like a person talking to me.

Ike: Did you obey that voice?

Bob: No I didn't obey and that was the worst journey of my life.

Ike: It's happened to me before, but now we know, let us listen to the Spirit.

LISTEN TO THE SPIRIT.

The body says, "Food, sleep, give me more sleep."
The Spirit says, "Plan, work, or tomorrow you'll weep."

The body says, "Buy now, spend now, nothing too cheap."
The Spirit says, "Save now, or tomorrow you'll be picking from the street."

The body says, "Cars, clothes, I need more."
The Spirit says, "That's enough for now, or tomorrow you'll be poor."

The body says, "Chips, burgers, give me without measure."
The Spirit says, "Not too often, or you will get high blood pressure."

The body says, "Cookies, cakes, fill the whole plate."
The Spirit says, "Take only one, before it is too late."

The body says, "Drink it all, have some more, make this night a blast."
The Spirit says, "If you continue this way, you'll be a memory of the past."

The body says, "Eat this, eat that, and take as much as you can."
The Spirit says, "Slow down now, so you don't reduce your lifespan."

The body says, "Take it, deny it, there is no harm."
The Spirit says, "Don't do that, you'll set off an alarm."

The body says, "Go here, go there, and go with your feet."
The Spirit says, "Don't go there; it's a dark and deadly street."

The body says, "Women, men, give me pleasure."
The Spirit says, "Wait, wait, don't give out your treasure."

The body says, "Go with the flow, when you are away from your spouse."
The Spirit says, "Avoid situations that will make you aroused."

The body says, "Do it for today, don't worry about tomorrow."
The Spirit says, "Your actions today may lead to tomorrow's sorrows."

The body says, "That's me, I know, I may lead you to destruction."
The Spirit says, "Obey me, my friend, follow my instruction."

The body says, "That's me, I know, I don't follow any rules."
The Spirit says, "Listen to me, my friend, I care about you."

Recommended Bible Reading: Romans 8

Obedience to the body can lead to destruction, but Obedience to the Spirit leads to life and peace.
Romans 8:6, (paraphrased).

If you think you are standing strong, be careful not to fall. The temptations in your life are no different from what others experience. And God is faithful. He will not allow the temptation to be more than you can stand. When you are tempted, he will show you a way out so that you can endure.
1 Corinthians 10:12-13,

Self-control is the ability to say no when no one is looking, even though you could say yes and no one would know; however, we all know that God knows. He's Omniscient (all knowing)

He Knows Everything

¹ O Lord, you have examined my heart and know everything about me.

² You know when I sit down or stand up. You know my thoughts even when I'm far away.

³ You see me when I travel and when I rest at home.
You know everything I do.

⁴ You know what I am going to say even before I say it, Lord.

⁵ You go before me and follow me. You place your hand of blessing on my head.

⁶ Such knowledge is too wonderful for me, too great for me to understand!

⁷ I can never escape from your Spirit!
I can never get away from your presence!

⁸ If I go up to heaven, you are there;
if I go down to the grave, you are there.

⁹ If I ride the wings of the morning,
if I dwell by the farthest oceans,

¹⁰ even there your hand will guide me, and your strength will support me.

¹¹ I could ask the darkness to hide me and the light around me to become night—

¹² but even in darkness I cannot hide from you. To you the night shines as bright as day. Darkness and light are the same to you.

Psalm 139: 1-12

The Holy Spirit is our Advantage

The Holy Spirit makes life comfortable for us. The Holy Spirit is not just something within you that tells you what's wrong. The Holy Spirit is a person. He guides, he speaks, he hears, he shows, he teaches, and he reminds us. He is our advantage. Jesus said,

> *But I tell you the truth, it is to your advantage that I go away; for if I do not go away, the Helper will not come to you; but if I go, I will send Him to you.*
> John 16:7, (New American Standard Bible).

How is the Holy Spirit our advantage?

1. The Holy Spirit helps us.

> *...the Holy Spirit helps us in our weakness…"*
> Romans 8:26

2. The Holy Spirit guides us.

> *When the Spirit of truth comes, he will guide you into all truth. He will not speak on his own but will tell you what he has heard. He will tell you about the future.*
> John 16:13

As a Christian, the Holy Spirit is your lifetime GPS.

Things to know about the Holy Spirit

1. He may give you an instruction that is not what you want to hear, but it is good for you.

For example, you arrive at a party and you just started having fun. Suddenly the Holy Spirit says, "There's danger ahead; leave the party." The best response is to leave.

2. He won't force you to do anything, but it is beneficial for you to obey him.

> *My Spirit will not struggle with humans…*
> Genesis 6: 3 (God's Word Translation).

3. He has a still small voice, so you need to be sensitive to hear him. Also, due to the softness of his voice, it is easy to ignore him. You may say to yourself, "That's not the Holy Spirit."

4. The Holy Spirit can be grieved, when you continuously disobey him.

> *And do not grieve the Holy Spirit …*
> Ephesians 4:30, (New International Version).

5. The Holy Spirit can be quenched; that means you lose the joy of his fellowship,

> *Do not quench the Spirit.*
> 1 Thessalonians 5:19 (New International Version)

It is possible to lose sensitivity to his voice because you have disobeyed him so much before. At this point, you no longer know the difference between his voice and any other voice.

Don't get tired of hearing and obeying the Holy Spirit's instruction. Don't take a break from the Holy Spirit and say, "Today, I am going to do what I want, when I want." It's dangerous.

It's Your Choice

When we were babies, we didn't have a choice about the clothes we wore, the foods we ate, or the places we went, but now, we are mature enough to make decisions. Your parents can't force you to do anything. Even if they say, "James, don't eat too many cookies," you could still buy cookies when you step out of the house, and they won't know. Just like a good parent, the Holy Spirit can only instruct you and remind you again and again and again... but he can't force you; however, you will face the consequences of your decisions.

Don't pack your bags and walk out on the Holy Spirit. Life would become very uncomfortable. We need the Holy Spirit.

Comic

Ike: I also describe the Holy Spirit as my faithful lawyer.
Bob: How much does he charge?
Ike: Nothing, all he requires is my obedience.

The Holy Spirit-My Faithful Lawyer

He goes before me, pleading in my favor;
He goes with me, telling me what to say;
He works hard for me every single day,
But he still doesn't ask me for any hourly pay.

He's a lawyer, indeed.
I cannot be deceived;
I have confidence in him
That's why I am so relieved.

He deals with my prayer requests-
He arranges them in clear cases,
Then he presents them in strategic phases
So they can appeal to the Judge (God), who doesn't look at faces.

There's a way to approach the Judge
His presentation is excellent.
There's a way to speak; his words are convincing:
He's my representative; he talks very well-
One word from me and he can make it sell.

Even though I make suggestions, I still stand at attention-
I don't rush him;
I wait for his direction.
He's my faithful lawyer-that's his profession.
He's been working for years,
But he doesn't have a pension.

. . . . ● . . . .

He pleads in our favor

And the Holy Spirit helps us in our weakness.
For example, we don't know what God wants us
to pray for. But the Holy Spirit prays for us with
groaning's that cannot be expressed in words.
Romans 8:26

Just like a lawyer in court, the Holy Spirit speaks on our behalf. He presents our case (prayers) to God (the Judge) and he pleads in our favor.

He tells us what to say

And when you are brought to trial in the synagogues
and before rulers and authorities, don't worry about
how to defend yourself or what to say, for the Holy Spirit
will teach you at that time what needs to be said.
Luke 12: 11-12

Just as a physical lawyer tells you, "When you get in court, say this…
or don't say that…" in the same way, the Holy Spirit can tell us what
to say at every point in time.

Heart to Heart

Ike: The Holy Spirit is also like a police officer to me.
Bob: Let me guess. He has arrested you before?
Ike: Yes, many times.

The Holy Spirit-My Police Officer

He stays awake guarding my life
He catches me, arrests me, but he never forgets me.
He restricts me, restrains me, but he never disgraces me.
Even when I thought he was gone because of what I did
He came back again to correct me.

He caught me when I was doing evil
He shouted, "Stop! That's plain uncivil."

He told me, "STOP! There's danger ahead."
I couldn't go forward; He showed me a new route instead
I didn't know the way but he directed my steps.

He tracks me down alone; He doesn't look for back-up
He knows where I will be, and He arrives before I mess up

He cautioned me when I was going too fast
He restrained me when I was out on a blast
"That's enough," He said, "you're making too much noise"
Unlike any officer He has a still, small voice.

He arrested me but nobody knew
All this happened before the police department had a clue
I gave my life to Christ, and everything became new

They don't know my name because
My police officer caught me before I was an object of shame
He's never late.

Physically, you cannot find Him,
That's because He's now inside me
I will never regret the day that He came to stay
He is my police officer
I enjoy fellowship with Him every day.

You are under arrest

The Holy Spirit is my police officer indeed. Before I surrendered my life to Jesus Christ, I was a very wild boy. Even after I gave my life to Christ the first time, I still went back to the old, bad habits. I lived recklessly from Monday till Saturday, but on Sunday I would go to church like nothing happened. I was even an usher in church.

One day the Holy Spirit arrested me. I went to church and the pastor preached a message that penetrated into my innermost being. Some of the statements mentioned (paraphrased):

"If you are not sure whether you are saved, then
you are not, come out and make sure,"

"You may have done it before, but you went
backwards, come out and make sure."

"If judgement day was today, ask yourself,
would you be going to Heaven or Hell?"

"It doesn't matter your title or your position in
the church, that doesn't make you saved."

"Some people around you may think you are saved
because of how you act in their presence, but you
know you are not saved, come out and make sure."

Don't be ashamed

The world may think you know God but you know that you don't
have a relationship with Him. The worse thing is to gain the approval
of human beings but be disapproved of by God. You could deceive
everyone else but you can't deceive yourself and you can't deceive
God. I came out to the altar to surrender my life to Christ with my
usher's tag around my neck. Although I was born into a Christian
family, I grew up going to church and I served in the church, none of
these activities meant that I was saved. I had to personally and boldly
declare Jesus as my Lord and personal savior.

*For it is by believing in your heart that you are
made right with God, and it is by confessing
with your mouth that you are saved.*
Romans 10:10

You can't be sitting on the fence any longer; you are either with God or against God. Choose God and His principles for life and you will never be ashamed.

"Anyone who trusts in him will never be disgraced."
Romans 10:11

Please say this prayer:

"Father, I know that I have broken your laws and my sins have separated me from you. I am truly sorry, and now I want to turn away from my past sinful life toward you. Please forgive me, and help me avoid sinning again. I believe that your son, Jesus Christ died for my sins, was resurrected from the dead, is alive, and hears my prayer. I invite Jesus to become the Lord of my life, to rule and reign in my heart from this day forward. Please send your Holy Spirit to help me obey You, and to do Your will for the rest of my life. In Jesus' name I pray, Amen." (Source: www.allaboutgod.com)

Congratulations, if you have prayed this prayer honestly you are now born again. Join a local church, be baptized, and continue to grow in the knowledge of God through His word, the Bible. You don't have to feel anything, just believe everything.

For we live by believing and not by seeing
2 Corinthians 5:7

Today marks a new beginning in your life. The best is yet to come. Congratulations!

HEART TO HEART

Bob: You've talked a lot about the Holy Spirit, and I know He's there but sometimes I find it difficult to hear what He's saying.

Ike: He's there but you couldn't hear him because you were not sensitive. The radio station could be on 24/7 but until you tune in you can't hear anything.

Bob: How do I tune in and increase my sensitivity?

Ike: One way I learned to increase my sensitivity to the Holy Spirit is by fasting.

Bob: So I should just go a whole day without food.

Ike: No, it doesn't have to be a whole day and fasting is more than just staying away from food.

FASTING

· · · · · · · · · · ● · · · · · · · · · · ·

Fasting refines and strengthens you–
Give it a try.
Fasting is so enlightening–
Trust me, you won't die.

Fasting is so empowering–
Say no to food for a while.
No one should know you are fasting:
Keep a bright smile.

Yes, it's discipline,
Staying focused in hunger.
It's the Spirit versus the body–
Show the body who's stronger!

Fasting is not punishment:
You're only denying yourself of food.
Be happy and be joyful–
Don't allow food to determine your mood.

You may be fasting today,
But your neighbor doesn't need to know.
Just focus on the purpose;
No need to make a show.

Even though there's no food in your stomach,
Don't leave your mouth to be smelly:
Brush your teeth and comb your hair;
Don't think about your belly.

One hour may seem long-
It may even feel like one day.
You said you wanted power:
This is the price to pay.

Fasting is not dieting-
Don't worry about losing weight.
Stay focused during this time;
Keep your mind away from the plate.

You are letting the Spirit take over,
And you are putting the body under.
It's almost 6' o clock-
You can wait a little longer.

You may feel hunger pains;
You may even have a light head.
Don't ruin this quality time
Because of a piece of bread.

Fasting is not just about going without food:
You should have specific goals-
Fasting without prayer
Is like putting money in pockets with holes.

Fasting helps us to focus:
It is done individually;
We do it for ourselves-
Completion is a sign of maturity.

It's not about how long but how well-
Don't worry about the time.
Prepare your own schedule-
Don't worry about mine.

Some people put aside food;
They do it with a smile,
But fasting is not only about food-
Put that thing you love aside for a while.

. . . . ● . . . .

Biblical fasting is putting aside food so you can grow spiritually. However, it is not only about putting aside food; it also involves putting those other things you love aside for a while, so you can spend time with God.

It is a time to:

- Say "*no*" to food and "*Yes!*" to God.
- Leave the plate and make a date with God.
- Fasten our flesh so we can fatten our spirit.
- Stand up in prayer, so we can stand out in life.
- Put the flesh under, so we can stay over in every area of life.
- Withdraw from food and draw near to God.
- Discipline ourselves in order to become acceptable disciples of Jesus.
- Put away the snack, so we can make sure that we are on the right track.

Please note:

Fasting is not designed to punish us but to polish us.

For more details on fasting and the benefits, recommended Bible reading: Isaiah 58.

It's a lifestyle

Fasting is not something you should do once and never again. To build your physical muscles, you don't go to the gym once a year; you go to the gym regularly. In the same way, to build your spiritual muscles, you don't fast once a year, you fast often. It is part of my schedule to fast at least once every week. Fasting doesn't kill. It is good for your spirit, and it is good for your body.

Your body needs regular physical exercise to stay healthy (e.g. running). Your Spirit needs regular spiritual exercise to stay healthy too (e.g. fasting and praying).

Physical training is good, but training for godliness is much better, promising benefits in this life and in the life to come."
1 Timothy 4:8

Personal Lessons Learned From Fasting:

- **Food is not my god**. I am not ruled by food. Food cannot control me. I am not living to eat; I am eating for strength to accomplish my daily tasks. There is more to life than eating and drinking (Matthew 4:4).
- **Prayer and fasting doesn't kill**. Some people think if they don't eat, they will die. You won't die. Fast and pray for one day, you'll discover that you are still alive and food will have no control over you.
- **Prayer and fasting leads to great revelations**. Every time I fast, I receive a fresh flow of inspiration and ideas. Things that I didn't understand before become a lot clearer. It's amazing. The fasting poem (above) was written while I was fasting. I had a rush of revelation, I started writing and I couldn't put my pen down.

- **Fasting enhances focus**. I used to find it difficult to read books and finish them, but fasting helped me to block out distractions. Food is a necessity; however, a lot of time can be wasted thinking about food, buying food, preparing food, and eating food. I can say with boldness that when I am fasting, I am more productive.
- **Fear can be defeated.** I used to be very fearful. I feared certain groups of people. I feared the unknown; however, through fasting and prayer, the spirit of boldness entered into me, and I am now walking with confidence.

> *For God has not given us a spirit of fear*
> *and timidity, but of power...*
> 2 Timothy 1:7

**"The devil wants you to keep eating and eating
so he can keep hitting and hitting you."**
(Bishop David Abioye)

When you are eating, you are weak. If you can control your appetite you can control your life.

HEART TO HEART

Bob: I know fasting is good, but sometimes, I can't focus. I get angry easily and I keep thinking about people who have hurt my feelings.

Ike: Before you start fasting or praying, you should forgive anyone who has hurt your feelings. Otherwise fasting and prayer may be a waste of time.

Bob: Okay.

Ike: A life of forgiveness is the best way to live. I heard someone say that before people offend him, he has forgiven them already.

Bob: I'll try that.

Ike: That's the way to live long and look young. Don't carry a heavy heart and a long face around. Forgive them, forget about what they did, and move on with life.

FORGIVE

So close yet so far
Even though we drive in the same car.

So close yet so far
I'm aggravated from afar.

So close yet so far
Even the way he opens the jar.

So close yet so far
Wish I could hit him with a bar.

So close yet so far
I was told to forget about that scar.

And whenever you stand praying, if you have anything against anyone, forgive him so that your Father in heaven may also forgive you your sins. But if you do not forgive, neither will your Father in heaven forgive your sins.
Mark 11: 25-26 (New King James Version)

Do not say, "I'll do to them as they have done to me; I'll pay them back for what they did"
Proverbs 24:29 (New International Version).

"I made an agreement with my wife that no argument continues after 24 hours."
(Chris Jumbo)

If someone slaps you on the right cheek, offer the other cheek also.
Matthew 5:39

Forgive and forget.

Dialogue: Continue to Forgive, Again, Again, and Again...

Son: Hello, Dad. Can I tell you something?

Dad: Sure, go ahead.

Son: There's this guy in school; he keeps stepping on my toes.

Dad: How many times did he step on your toes?

Son: Three times.

Dad: Son, you should be willing to forgive him; he probably made a mistake.

Son: How many more times do I have to forgive him?

Dad: At least seven times.

Son: (2 weeks later) Dad, he stepped on my toes four more times. That makes seven. I think it's time to fight him.

Dad: Son, remember when you asked me how many times you should forgive?

Son: Yes.

Dad: I didn't give you the correct answer. Sorry. I saw in the Bible that Peter had the same question as you.

Dad: Matthew 18:21-22 says that Peter asked, "Lord, how often should I forgive someone who sins against me? Seven times?" and Jesus replied, "No, not seven times, but seventy times seven!"

(Son starts to calculate… 7 x 7 is 49, add another 0…)

Dad: Son, don't worry about the calculation; God is telling us that we should always forgive.

HEART TO HEART

Bob: What if I forgive them now and they do something bad again?

Ike: Keep doing good to them even if they do badly to you. This principle has helped me to solve many problems.

Bob: How?

Ike: Goodness is contagious.

GOODNESS IS
CONTAGIOUS

He says shut up–
I say okay;
He says sit down–
I just obey.
I look at him–
He turns away,
But I still say, "Hello"
Every single day.

He walked away
When I came to stay;
I cooked him rice
But he threw it away.
Here we are
Yet another day.

He hates it when
I chew and crunch;
He throws a punch
But I still cook lunch.

Whatever he would do
Didn't change my mood,
Soon he discovered
And he said something good-
The good in me changed his attitude.

"Hello," he said,
"How are you today?"
God changed his heart
And now he's here to stay.

* * * * * * * * * * ● * * * * * * * * * * *

*Don't repay evil for evil. Don't retaliate with
insults when people insult you. Instead, pay
them back with a blessing. That is what God has
called you to do, and he will bless you for it.*
1 Peter 3:9

Bless those who curse you, pray for those who mistreat you
Luke 6: 28 (New International Version).

So let's not get tired of doing what is good
Galatians 6:9

Let Us Follow Jesus' Example

If we look at how Jesus dealt with unbelievers, we have a real example
of how we should act. Jesus had many enemies. They slapped him, but
he didn't retaliate. He would have still protected them. They spat on
him, but he would have still given them drink when they were thirsty.
They stole from him, but he would still share his food with them.
They tried to kill him, but he laid down his life for them.

*If your enemy is hungry, feed him; if he is
thirsty, give him something to drink...*
Romans 12:20, New International Version

*Never pay back evil with more evil.
Do things in such a way that everyone
can see you are honorable.
Do all that you can to live in peace with everyone.*
Romans 12:17-18

Don't let evil conquer you, but conquer evil by doing good
Romans 12:21

**I didn't fight him today because I knew that we
would be friends tomorrow, and I didn't want
to stop that from happening. Today, I can sit,
laugh and have an educated discussion with the
same person who didn't want to see my face.**

How fights start

Tim: Hey, why did you just step on my shoe? You blind goat!
John: What did you say? You dumb cow!
Tim: Your Mamma!
John: Your Grandmamma!
Tim: (Hit!)
John: (Hit!)

The fight starts!

How to stop a fight before it starts.

It only takes one person; you can be that person.

Tim: Hey, why did you just step on my shoe? You blind goat!

John: Oh, sorry. It was an accident. (Walks away)

Stranger: Did you just hear what he called you? He called you blind and he called you a goat!

John: Ok.

Stranger: Why didn't you fight him? We would have helped you.

John: I didn't fight him because I woke up this morning and I didn't see horns on my head or a tail attached to me.

Stranger: So, what does that mean?

John: Goats have horns and a tail. I'm not a goat. He wasn't talking to me so I don't need to be offended. Only a blind goat should be offended.

HEART TO HEART

Ike: I learned that I should love my neighbour as myself.

Bob: But, in your goat example before, Tim was really pushing it.

Ike: Sometimes, we just have to be patient. One way to demonstrate our love for each other is to try and understand each other. Tim might be having a stressful day.

Bob: Hmm…okay.

Ike: Another way to show our love for each other is by giving, especially to people in need.

HELP THOSE IN NEED

You see them and you walk;
You always have time to mock.
You hear, but you don't talk-
Just help, stop looking at your clock.

Offer help to the needy;
Send food to the hungry.
Your wardrobe is full of clothes-
They don't even have laundry.

Support, help, and lend-
Pick up their slack,
Take the responsibility,
Don't turn your back.

Don't worry about the amount-
It's the thought that counts;
Give, Give, Give!
You'll have more in your account.

Do it from your heart;
Don't worry about fame.
Give with a smile;
Don't ask for anything in exchange.

Opportunity, Ability, and Grace

My regular prayer request is:

Lord, give me the opportunity, ability, and the grace to give.

This is a very specific prayer and all three components are needed. The opportunity to give is relatively constant because there are less fortunate people everywhere.

> **There will always be some in the land who**
> **are poor. That is why I am commanding**
> **you to share freely with the poor...**
> Deuteronomy 15: 11

The ability to give is needed because a person can't give what they don't have. Although we have the opportunity and the ability, we need the grace to give. We need grace to willingly release what we have to another person.

Give in secret and your reward will be open.

> **When you give to someone in need, don't do as the**
> **hypocrites do-blowing trumpets in the synagogues and**
> **streets to call attention to their acts of charity! I tell you the**
> **truth; they have received all the reward they will ever get.**
> Matthew 6:2

> **Give your gifts in private, and your Father,**
> **who sees everything, will reward you.**
> Matthew 6:4

Do they want money or food?

It is very important to be spiritual in our approach to giving. Don't go throwing money to whoever you see because you don't know if you're funding someone's negative addiction. If someone asks you for money, kindly ask them what they need the money for. If it is food, or something else within reach (e.g. a bus pass), buy them the product, and don't give them the money.

Why do I say this? One day I was at the train station and a woman approached me and told me that she missed her train and she needs money to buy a new ticket. In my opinion, she appeared genuine. I gave her money. About 6 months later, I was passing through the same train station, and behold, this same woman approached me. It was clear that she didn't remember me, but I clearly remembered her. I paused for a second to let her speak. She said, "You won't guess what just happened to me…" That was her special introduction, but she didn't expect to tell the story to the same person twice. I didn't allow her to finish before I said to her "I think I've met you before…" Judging from her deteriorated appearance, I perceived that she was using the money to satisfy her addiction. This experience taught me a significant lesson. Be sensitive in the Spirit at all times and don't tempt people to misuse money by giving them physical cash.

Create your Opportunities

Therefore, whenever we have the opportunity,
we should do good to everyone…
Galatians 6: 10

Many of us have the ability and the grace to give but we may not see the opportunity to give. In this case, we should look for opportunities. You don't need to wait for someone to ask you, "Please could you buy me…?" while you can see that they are in need. For example, you keep seeing this same man carrying all his books in his hand, and you can see that he probably can't afford a bag. This is an opportunity for you to bless him. Buy him a bag. Look out for opportunities around you. I made it a duty to give something to someone in need every week. If it gets to Saturday and I haven't given anything to anyone yet, I search for opportunities.

Always be prepared

Sometimes I carry extra food with me, in addition to my own food because I want to give to someone. I call this intentional giving. I say to myself while I am preparing my food, "When I am going to eat this sandwich, someone may want a taste". Rather than grumble at their request, I make an extra sandwich so we can both be satisfied.

*The generous will prosper; those who refresh
others will themselves be refreshed*
Proverbs 11: 25

Prosperity Mentality leads to Prosperity Actuality

If you want to be rich you must first change your mentality. Think rich. Desire opportunities to help others. Think of ways you can help humanity. This is the way forward.

Prosperity thoughts:

- I want to build churches for the advancement of the Kingdom of God.
- I am tired of seeing people struggling to get to church. I want to buy cars for them.
- Lord, when you give me the ability, I will give scholarships to students so they can go to school.

It is true that you may not have much money but as you start thinking rich and you start trading the little you have, it will come back to you as much. What do I mean by trade? The Bible says:

Give, and you will receive. Your gift will return to you in full--pressed down, shaken together to make room for more, running over, and poured into your lap. The amount you give will determine the amount you get back.
Luke 6:38

Everything you currently possess is a seed. Every seed has the potential to be a tree with many fruits. However, the seed will never be a tree until you plant the seed.

Remember this—a farmer who plants only a few seeds will get a small crop. But the one who plants generously will get a generous crop.
2 Corinthians 9:6

Giving is spiritual planting which guarantees a wealthy future for you. As long as you keep giving, you will keep receiving. Keep giving more and will keep receiving more. The cycle will continue because *"as long as the earth remains, there will be planting and harvest, cold and heat, summer and winter, day and night."* Genesis 8:22. This is God's guarantee to you.

Heart to Heart

Ike: I know what you're thinking, why me?
Bob: Yes, why do I have to help them?
Ike: Like everything in life, it's a choice. But there are blessings attached to this choice.

Your Blessing is closer than you think.

· · · · · · · · · · · · · · ◉ · · · · · · · · · · · · ·

Giving, me.
Cleaning, me.
Serving, me.
Why always me?

Working, me.
Caring, me.
Loving, me.
Why always me?
Why not him?
Why not you?

I chose you
Because I have great plans for you;
If you are not interested,
I'll choose someone new.

If you don't want the opportunity,
You can't have the reward-
Only committed servants
Will get the award.

Don't be tired of doing good;
Your reward is getting closer:
You'll have it very soon.

· · · · · · · · · · · · · · ◉ · · · · · · · · · · · · ·

Read the following passages and allow them to sink in. These are not my words, these are God's words:

Freely you have received; freely give
Matthew 10:8 (New International Version).

...What do you have that God hasn't given you?
And if everything you have is from God,
why boast as though it were not a gift?
1 Corinthians 4:7

Share each other's burdens. . . If you think you are too
important to help someone, you are only fooling yourself.
You are not that important.
Galatians 6:2-3

If you help the poor, you are lending to the LORD—
and he will repay you!
Proverbs 19:17

...For I was hungry, and you fed me. I was thirsty,
and you gave me a drink. I was a stranger, and
you invited me into your home. I was naked, and
you gave me clothing. I was sick, and you cared
for me. I was in prison, and you visited me.
Then these righteous ones will reply, "Lord, when
did we ever see you hungry and feed you? Or thirsty
and give you something to drink? Or a stranger
and show you hospitality? Or naked and give you
clothing? When did we ever see you sick or in prison
and visit you?" And the King will say, "I tell you the
truth, when you did it to one of the least of these my
brothers and sisters, you were doing it to me!"
Matthew 25:35-40

The blessings of giving…

*Give generously to the poor, not grudgingly, for the Lord
your God will bless you in everything you do. There will
always be some in the land who are poor. That is why I
am commanding you to share freely with the poor…*
Deuteronomy 15: 10-11

Whoever gives to the poor will lack nothing . . .
Proverbs 28:27

*Give and you will receive. Your gift will
return to you in full--pressed down, shaken
together to make room for more,
running over, and poured into your lap . . .*
Luke 6:38

*. . . Let's not get tired of doing what is good. At just the
right time we will reap a harvest of blessing if we don't
give up. Therefore, whenever we have the opportunity,
we should do good to everyone*
Galatians 6: 9-10

HEART TO HEART

Bob: It's true, we all need endurance.

Ike: I agree. In every area of life we need endurance. Our reward is coming soon, let's not turn back now, we've come too far.

ENDURE

Endure the pain-
Your work is not in vain:
You may struggle tonight,
But tomorrow there's great gain.

You are not lame-
Today may bring shame;
Problems only last a moment:
Tomorrow won't be the same.

...One may experience sorrow during the night,
but joy arrives in the morning
Psalm 30:5 (New English Translation Bible).

We can rejoice, too, when we run into problems and trials,
for we know that they help us develop endurance.
And endurance develops strength of character,
and character strengthens our confident hope
Romans 5: 3-4

The fact that you have fallen once doesn't mean
that life must stop. You can always rise up again!
(Bishop David Abioye)

Every time you feel more pressure, it is an
indication that you are closer to your miracle.
That is when you should press harder.
(Bishop Abioye, rephrased).

Heart to Heart

Ike: The prize is given to those who endure till the end of the race.
Bob: I agree.
Ike: It doesn't matter how you started, you can always get better and
win in the end.

I will get better.

- - - - - - - - - - - - ●- - - - - - - - - - - -

I will receive.
I will achieve.
Whether you agree or not,
I will believe.

More math's homework-
Pile it on the plate.
It may take a while,
But I'll make the due date.

Don't pity me; I am happy-there's no sorrow.
Learning is a process; it will be easier tomorrow.

To those that mock me, and burst into laughter-
It doesn't bother me because it's what I say that matters.

You got an A grade; I'm happy for you, it's lovely.
But I will soon be the loudest in the class and it will be hard to ignore me.

- - - - - - - - - - - - ●- - - - - - - - - - - -

From the Bottom to the Top

In high school, mathematics was not one of my strongest subjects. I was in Set 3 for mathematics, which was equivalent to the bottom rank of the class. My father gave me some advice. He said, "In school, you may be good at some subjects but not so good at others. To succeed, you need to identify people who are strong in the subjects where you are weak and study with them." To admit that you need help requires a lot of modesty. I was ready to take this step. I can deceive everyone else, but I can't deceive myself. I needed help so I searched for it. I refused to settle for failure. On many occasions, I stayed back after school to study. I was ready to do all it takes to succeed in math.

Our math classes were divided into sets to accommodate every student's learning speed. Set 1, Set 2, and Set 3 students were taught in separate rooms. Set 1 and Set 2 students were seen as "the top students," but I wasn't disturbed. My eyes were fixed on my ultimate goal, an A grade in math. Interestingly, we all took the same final exam at the end of the year. So, however you choose to get to the finish line is up to you, but the final results will show who was working or joking. Glory be to God; I got an A as my final grade.

Lessons Learned:

- Wherever talent won't take you, hard work can get you there.
- Hard working individuals will catch up to talented individuals and overtake them if talented individuals are not working hard. (Sir Alex Ferguson, Former Manager, Manchester United Football Club, quote paraphrased).
- From my experience as a soccer player, some coaches prefer to put hard working players ahead of talented players because they understand that it is not the talented team that wins, it is the hardworking team.
- Talent may take you to the top but hard work will keep you there. If you don't work hard, a harder worker will displace you.

HEART TO HEART

Bob: It seems like teamwork really helped you during your studies.

Ike: Certainly, I value teamwork. John Maxwell said "Teamwork makes the dream work."

Bob: A one-man team will never win.

Ike: You're right. While playing soccer in college, I also learned that a team of average players who work together will beat a team of talented players who are individuals on the field.

TEAMWORK

Let your light shine for all to see-
There's a gift in you; there's a gift in me.
Let's get together; we'll make a great team.

One can only do so much; one can do so little.
Let's put our minds together, and solve this world's issues.
If you go alone, you may hit a stone-
Let me go with you; I'll be your backbone.

There's a lot more to achieve.
Let us have faith and believe.
There's a jewel in you and a jewel in me:
Let's get together and let us dream.

By yourself, it's as far as you can see,
But stand on my shoulders and you'll see beyond that tree.
Teamwork is good; it creates healthy conversation.
One can move a city, but two will move a nation.

Why are you in confusion?
While we have the solution-
Two can make a vision real,
But one may live an illusion.

There's a star in you;
There's a star in me.
Me plus you, our strength is infinity.
Partner with me; let's move with certainty.
I assure you, we'll make a landmark for eternity.

· · · · · · · · · · · · ◉ · · · · · · · · · · · ·

Heart to Heart

Bob: One is limited, two is unlimited.
Ike: It's true; we need people, in sports, in marriage, and in life.
There is no self-made person.

We Need People

· · · · · · · · · · · · ◉ · · · · · · · · · · · ·

A one-man team will never win.
A self-centered heart can never go far.
You can't run alone; you will soon get tired.
If you don't invest in people, your legacy will expire.

When the weight gets heavy, you must carry it alone,
But if you have two people, you can both share the load.
The job is simple; just add a few people.

No spouse in the house;
No children running about-
Loneliness is no good;
You will soon hear the mouse.

Wealth here and there, but who is there to share?
I prefer to have close people than money everywhere.

The larger share can't be compared
With the joy another person brings to the atmosphere.
The race is longer with one, but shorter with two.
Where would we be today if we didn't have people?

* *

⁹ Two people are better off than one, for they can help each other succeed.
¹⁰ If one person falls, the other can reach out and help. But someone who falls alone is in real trouble.
¹¹ Likewise, two people lying close together can keep each other warm. But how can one be warm alone?
¹² A person standing alone can be attacked and defeated, but two can stand back-to-back and conquer. Three are even better, for a triple-braided cord is not easily broken.

Ecclesiastes 4:9-12

HEART TO HEART

Bob: So you played soccer while studying, you were a tutor, and you were the president of a club on campus. How did you do all that?

Ike: I try to manage my time and plan ahead.

Bob: I need to make the most of my 24 hours in a day.

Ike: I'm glad you mentioned that. I will tell you a story about a man who inspired me.

THERE IS A TIME FOR EVERYTHING

He's a son to Hailey,
A father to Amy,
A brother to Jamie-
These are his responsibilities daily.

He's a friend to Tom;
He also has a son:
One son and two daughters
And there's one more boy to come.

He's a teacher in the morning;
He's a student in the night.
He goes to church on Sunday morning
Then he runs his business at twilight.

Twice a week, he's on the lookout,
Trying to stop crime.
He cooks, he cleans, and he cares-
He works hard for every dime.

There are 24 hours in a day;
Where does he get the time?
He's a man with many hats,
But he puts on one at a time.

. . . . ● . . . .

For everything there is a season, a
time for every activity...
Ecclesiastes 3:1

It's okay to be busy, but be busy with a purpose. Don't be a jack of all trades and a master of none.

Caution: It is better to do a few things very well, than to do many things not so well.

There was a man who wanted to build a house. When he looked into his bank account, he said, "I have enough money to build many houses in different countries." So he hired builders and he started seven houses in seven different countries. He didn't have time to monitor these building projects. After 5 years, he went to visit each country and he expected to stay in his completed houses. To his surprise, he discovered that none of them were finished. One of the builders admitted, "Sir, there was no one to encourage or motivate us to get the job done quickly so we were relaxed on the job." The man was forced to stay in a hotel and he became very sad. He was a rich man, but he didn't have a house of his own because he didn't give enough attention to one specific house.

Imagine if this man concentrated on one or two houses?

Lessons Learned:

- Don't put your hands in everything because you may end up achieving nothing! Focus on a few things at a time. Give it your best!
- It's one thing to invest money but if you don't invest the time to know how that money is being spent, your money may go to waste.

HEART TO HEART

Bob: I wish I was as lucky as that man with many hats.

Ike: I really don't like that word *luck*.

Bob: Why?

Ike: I believe that we all have equal opportunity to be great in our lifetimes. The difference is, some people take their opportunities and some people don't. Over the next few chapters, I'm going to get a little direct.

Bob: Saving the best till last, are you?

Ike: Not really. Everything in this book is very important. But I can't leave you without these final chapters.

GRAB YOUR OPPORTUNITIES

Opportunities come; opportunities go.
Take this one and others will follow.
Success is not cheap; it will require your labor.
Take this opportunity, or it will go to your neighbor.
Many saw opportunities and ignored: it didn't look real.
Two months later, they discovered it was the real deal.
It's right here; don't stand and stare.
Reach out and grab it; take your full share.
Opportunities are out there, for whoever wants them.
Some people wish and wait; only a few truly grab them.

Don't look down on small opportunities

- There was a woman called Rebecca who was educated and talented, but she was unemployed. A multi-million dollar company approached her and asked her, "Do you want a temporary job cleaning toilets?" She saw this as an opportunity--not an embarrassment--and she accepted the job. Some people would have said, "Me, cleaner? Never!"
- One month later, the manager said, "You have been very consistent at your job; you can start cleaning cafeterias only."

- Two months later, he said, "You are doing a good job. You are promoted. You can start cleaning the executive offices."
- She was amazed!
- Three months later, the manager said, "You are doing a great job. I think we need to hire you as a permanent staff member."
- The opportunity she saw initially was gradually becoming a reality.
- Four months later, she was promoted again. She became the leading cleaner and her wages increased.
- Five months later, her job description changed. The manager said, "No more cleaning for you; you will be in the Human Resources Department, recruiting and selecting cleaners for us."
- Six months later, the company changed its structure because it needed to expand. The business separated some departments into individual companies. The cleaning department became a separate entity.
- Rebecca received a letter which said:

Dear Rebecca,

We are extremely impressed by your progress during the last six months. Since you came into this business, you have been committed and consistent. On this day, July 1st, the beginning of the seventh month--we have decided to honor you. Due to the increasing demand for our cleaning services, we have decided to separate the cleaning department into a separate organization. You have been selected as the CEO (Chief Executive Officer) of the cleaning company. We would like you to choose the name of the business, the structure, and create the rules. We made this decision because we believe that you are the right person for the job, and based on your spotless work ethic, we know that you will not disappoint us. You are in charge. See this as your own company. Congratulations!

Yours Sincerely,

Joseph Peters
Your former Manager

> **"Our stepping stones in life come in the
> form of opportunities. Life's bonuses
> come in the form of opportunities."**
> (Bishop David Abioye)

> **"The opportunities that come your way
> determine your rate of growth. Every
> greatness is a product of opportunity."**
> (Bishop David Abioye)

> **"Opportunity is the promoter and agent of change.
> Every change is a result of utilized opportunity.
> A change of job, position, and marriage are
> all responses to various opportunities."**
> (Bishop David Abioye)

We have left the era of experience. We are in the era of the greatest opportunity. It's not the most skilled or the most experienced people who are becoming rich, it's the people who take their opportunities!

We have left the era that proclaimed "money is only in the hands of parents." Today, some high school students are millionaires because they utilized their opportunities. They can now say "Thanks mum and dad for the $10 and the financial advice; I brought $10,000 back. Please accept my gift."

Opportunities have wings; they can fly! When opportunities come to you and you don't take them, they will go to someone else. Bishop David Oyedepo (founder and president of Winner Chapel Worldwide), said that if he had not responded to the opportunity when God called him into ministry, someone else would have. The church in Lagos, Nigeria, seats over 50,000 people. He said, "Someone else would have initiated the building of this 50,000 capacity church."

Heart to Heart

Bob: I understand what you mean by opportunities but isn't it better to wait for the opportunity to come, then start getting ready?

Ike: Do soldiers wait for war before they start training?

Bob: No.

Ike: They live ready and so should we. Don't wait for opportunities: prepare for them, so when they come, you can take full advantage straight away.

Ike: Before we go into the next chapter, I want to share this personal testimony with you.

I Was Prepared

From a young age, I was passionate about football (soccer) and I wanted to play at a higher level, but I knew that I needed to improve. I trained regularly-in the sun, in the rain, and even in the snow. I took advantage of every opportunity to play soccer. Even if my friends didn't come to the field, I would go on my own. I remember those lonely days on the soccer field, asking myself, "When will my breakthrough come?"

I went for many tryouts, but I was not accepted. I didn't see it as rejection; rather, I saw it as feedback, which would help me to prepare for the next opportunity. I learned from my mistakes. I continued to practice. I knew something good was coming, but I didn't know when. I was working hard for something I couldn't see physically, but I could see it with my eyes of faith. Suddenly, a great opportunity came to study and play soccer in America. Dreams come true. I love studying and I love soccer, now I can do both at a higher level. Everything happened so fast, but I thank God because I was prepared. All those days on the soccer field were not a waste. On the day of the tryout, I knew that I was fit and ready to play. I stepped up to the task and I was accepted.

Success doesn't just come by accident, you must
prepare for it. If you are not prepared when
the opportunity comes, it will pass by.

It's better to be prepared for an opportunity
and not have one than to have an
opportunity and not be prepared.

(Les Brown)

HEART TO HEART

Bob: Let me guess, you've got a poem about preparation too?

Ike: Yes.

Bob: I knew it.

PREPARE

Prepare for your time;
It's drawing near.
The day may be far,
But preparation starts here.

The opportunity may be clear,
But don't wait-prepare.
Develop yourself now
So you can be ready when it's here.

Wait for your time;
It's drawing near.
Don't jump the gun,
So you don't shed tears.

Success is not by accident,
As some people may declare.
If you don't prepare now,
You may be waiting for years.

God is waiting for you

Many people are waiting for God, while God is waiting for them. They say in their hearts, "God, if you are there, why aren't you working?" The main question we should ask ourselves is, "Why am I not working?" God's part of the contract is sure:

I will not break my covenant;
I will not take back a single word I said.
Psalm 89:34

But we need to do our part. **Preparation is our part to play.**

People do the planning (preparing),
but the end result is from the Lord.
Proverbs 16:1 (International Standard Version)

DIAGRAM:

Your part to play →MIRACLE← God's part to play

We have to meet God in the middle by preparing. Do your best and God will do the rest! However, some people pray, wish, and wait, but they don't prepare. They want their miracle to fall from heaven and land in their hands while they do nothing for themselves. That's not how it works.

"Faith does not just say, 'God will do it.'
Faith says, 'What must I do to commit
God to do what He has promised?'"
(Bishop David Abioye)

There is always something for you to do. You must share responsibility and do your part while God does His part.

"You can't be confessing that God will bless you
with the best job and then sit down at home.
After you have prayed in the night, wake up in
the morning and say, 'Lord, direct my footsteps
today.' Then step out to look for a job."
(Bishop David Abioye)

"Any prayer that makes God 100% responsible for
the answer is an irresponsible prayer."
(Bishop David Oyedepo)

God Doesn't Lie

God is saying to us, "My children, your miracle is waiting for you; prepare, work, and you will get the breakthrough you want. I can't go back on my word because that would make me a liar and I am not a liar."

*God is not a man, so he does not lie. He is not human, so he
does not change his mind. Has he ever spoken and failed
to act? Has he ever promised and not carried it through?*
Numbers 23:19

The answer is NO!

God is not slow; if anything, we (humans) are the ones who are too slow.

*The Lord isn't really being slow about his promise,
as some people think. No, he is being patient for your
sake. He does not want anyone to be destroyed.*
2 Peter 3:9

God cannot take you higher than you are prepared for. He doesn't want to destroy you.

Consider this example: As a child, your parents bought you a new car but they won't give you the car keys until you are a certain age. They are keeping the keys because they love you. You won't get the car until you pass your driving test because your parents don't want you to kill yourself. You must know how to drive before you get the car.

Son, You're Not Ready

Son: Hello, Dad. Our family business is doing well. I am so excited about working here.

Dad: Yes, son, we've grown since last year.

Son: Have you filled that vacant position?

Dad: Which position?

Son: The Director of Human Resource Management.

Dad: Oh, that position! No, I haven't. We are still looking for the right person. Why do you ask? Do you know someone?

Son: Yes.

Dad: Who?

Son: Me. I know I have only worked for a couple of months, but I think I can handle it.

Dad: Son, you're only 18 years old; although age is not a barrier to promotion, I don't think you are ready for that role.

Son: Okay... (sighs)

Dad: I could put you there if I wanted because you are mature, but you still need to acquire more knowledge about Human Resource Management. I don't want you to be confused and lose interest in your job.

Son: Okay. I understand.

Dad: Son, can I ask you a question?

Son: Yes.

Dad: What's your last name?

Son: James.

Dad: What's the name of this business?

Son: James and Sons Manufacturers, since 1880.

Dad: Son, this is your company for life, but I don't want you to occupy any management position yet, so no one will trick you. When you acquire the relevant knowledge and I feel that you are prepared, you will get promoted. Deal?

Son: Deal! Thanks, Dad.

The blessing is yours, but you can't get it until you are prepared.

> *Think of it this way. If a father dies and leaves an inheritance for his young children, those children are not much better off than slaves until they grow up, even though they actually own everything their father had. They have to obey their guardians until they reach whatever age their father set.*
> Galatians 4:1-2

As you prepare, have faith in God

What is Faith?

> *Faith is the confidence that what we hope for will actually happen; it gives us assurance about things we cannot see.*
> Hebrews 11:1

You've not seen it yet (e.g. a job), but you know it's going to come; you are very sure, and you act as if you have your job already. This is faith. So while you are preparing:

1. Think success.
2. Talk success (e.g. I'm employed, I'm an A student, I'm a successful business man, I'm married, etc.).

3. Act like a success (e.g. Iron your suit and walk with your head up).
4. Very soon you will be a success.

A Few Notes on Preparation

- **Preparation is personal.** Nobody can eat for you; in the same way, no one can prepare for you. Even identical twins have to prepare individually. Preparation for some people is getting their resumes, CV's and business cards ready. For some people, it is buying their wedding dresses even though no man has approached them for marriage. For others, it is training and development. Just as our faces are all different, what we need to do to prepare is also different.
- **The time of preparation may be lonely.** It may seem like everybody else is having fun and you're the only one working. You're not the only one who feels that way. I wrote this book alone in my room. I had to separate myself from a lot of temporary pleasures, which would not have added value to my life in the long run. It was a sacrifice that I had to make.
- **There is a time to prepare and a time to perform.** There is a time to prepare and there is a time to enjoy the benefits of your preparation.

Consider this example:

In competitive sports, before teams compete, they engage in a time of pre-season training. It involves a lot of fitness exercises. Some athletes fear pre-season because they know they will be pushed beyond their limits. However, they know it is temporary pain with a future gain. The way in which a team approaches its pre-season training will have a major impact on its competitive season. So there's a time to practice (prepare) and a time to perform. Prepare now so you can give a great performance.

Prior planning promotes proper performance, presentation, passion, play, pray and pay.
(Source: http://simmymart.blogspot.com)

In his kindness God called you to share in his eternal glory by means of Christ Jesus. So after you have suffered a little while, he will restore, support, and strengthen you, and he will place you on a firm foundation.
1 Peter 5:10

These hard times are small potatoes compared to the coming good times, the lavish celebration prepared for us.
2 Corinthians 4:17, (The Message)

HEART TO HEART

Ike: While you are preparing, Stay focused.

Bob: How?

Ike: Don't compare yourself with others. Run your own race, and stay in your lane. Don't get distracted by what anyone else is doing.

RUN YOUR OWN RACE

Run your own race:
Stay in your lane;
Don't get distracted.
Everyone's doing the same.

Only look ahead:
Don't worry about who's who.
Why are you trying to copy him?
He's not even looking at you.

Don't compare yourself with others;
Do not feel ashamed.
You are created for a purpose;
You are not lame.

Stay in your lane:
Play smart and be wise;
Stay focused on your goals;
Keep your eyes on the prize.

He is successful; why?
Because he is running his own race,
He found his event on time
And fastened his shoe lace.

Learn from him-
His name is Jim.
Don't compete with him;
You won't win.

He's good at what he does-
Cooking lunch and supper.
Don't open your restaurant;
You won't make a dollar.

Jack of all trades
Doesn't take you too far;
You are here today and there tomorrow-
Life becomes a roller coaster.

The beginning may be sweet,
The middle even sweeter;
Suddenly there's a crash-
The end is very bitter.

He is making money today,
But that doesn't stop you.
You are very unique;
You are good at what you do.

Run your own race;
Do what you are created to do.
Be patient:
The world will soon notice you.

You are created for a purpose. You were not born by accident. There is a reason you are living.

God said, "Before I made you in your mother's
womb, I chose you. Before you were born,
I set you apart for a special work."
Jeremiah 1:5 (New Century Version)

We are set apart for a special work. A special work could also mean a special race.

What is My Race? What am I Created For?

The race of life is like the Olympic Games. In the Olympic Games, there are many different races and events: the 100-meter, 200-meter, 400-meter, 10,000-meter, javelin throw, long jump, etc. It is common to see that one individual athlete specializes in one particular race. They may be able to compete in other races, but there is one specific race which they can confidently say "this is my race."

- In the same way, God has given each of us a race. This is the race where we will experience the most fulfillment. This is our purpose.
- Your purpose could be in teaching, business, nursing, sports etc. God has a plan for your life. Once you've identified your purpose, stay there!
- Let everyone stay in the race God put them in (1 Corinthians 7:20, paraphrased).

And let us run with endurance the
race God has set before us.
Hebrews 12:1

How Do I Discover My Purpose?

One way to discover your purpose is to ask God. You might say, "Lord, what is your plan for me? What did you create me for?" He will tell you!

Call to me and I will answer you, and I will tell you
great and hidden things that you have not known.
Jeremiah 33:3 (English Standard Version).

Some people may think, "I can run this race well, so this must be my race." Don't decide for yourself; ask God. Just because you can do something well doesn't mean you should do it. If you notice above, I said that the race God gives you is the race where you will find the most fulfillment. It may not be the race where you think you are the best. Interestingly, in your eyes, you may not be good at the race God has called you to run, but there is a great future for you there. Why? God said so.

Don't consider your weaknesses

God gave Moses an assignment and he considered his weaknesses:

> *But Moses pleaded with the Lord, "O Lord, I'm not*
> *very good with words. I never have been, and I'm not*
> *now, even though you have spoken to me. I get*
> *tongue-tied, and my words get tangled."*
>
> *Then the Lord asked Moses, "Who makes a person's*
> *mouth? Who decides whether people speak or do not*
> *speak, hear or do not hear, see or do not see? Is it not*
> *I, the Lord? Now go! I will be with you as you*
> *speak, and I will instruct you in what to say."*
> Exodus 4:10-12

When God calls you to a race, don't worry, He will give you all you need to finish the race successfully.

"If natural qualifications were to be considered, I would have been the most unlikely candidate for a preaching

ministry. I was very slow-tongued and also very sickly, but God called me and that made the difference."
(Bishop David Oyedepo)

Paul had a similar testimony.

My grace is all you need. My power
works best in weakness.
So now I am glad to boast about my weaknesses,
so that the power of Christ can work through me.
That's why I take pleasure in my weaknesses…
For when I am weak, then I am strong.
2 Corinthians 12:9-10

Grace makes the difference

If **G**od is in your **race**, you've got the **Grace!** That's all you need.

The grace of God was working for Paul; that is why he could say:

But by God's grace I am what I am, and his grace shown to
me was not wasted. Instead, I worked harder than all the
others—not I, of course, but God's grace that was with me.
1 Corinthians 15:10 (International Standard Version)

Don't compare yourself with others

Everyone's race is different. Don't compare yourself with other people. No one's success can stop your success because we are all in different races. Could you imagine a runner saying, "Oh, no, that swimmer just won his race; I have no chance of winning mine." Sounds funny, doesn't it? That's how funny it is if you try to compare yourself with another person. It doesn't matter if it looks like your friends and relatives are ahead in their own race (e.g., good grades, good job, and good car). Be patient in your own race.

Different Races, Different Distances

A 100-meter race and a 10,000-meter race may start at the same time, but due to the distance of the race, the 100-meter finishes first. But that doesn't make the 10,000-meter runner slow or a loser! So, when you see others succeeding, don't look down on yourself. Don't say "Look at where he is up there and look at where I am down here, and we both graduated together. Life is not fair." Don't allow those thoughts to settle in your mind and don't let those words come out of your mouth. You can succeed and you will succeed if you don't give up. It's just a matter of time. In the end, you will celebrate together!

Your time is coming

James and John are best friends, but they work in two different companies. James gets paid every week, while John gets paid every month. Due to the nature of his job, James can see the immediate rewards of his work every week, while John has to wait the whole month. Although James is paid more frequently, there is no reason for John to feel inferior to his friend because John knows that he will be paid at the end of the month. In the same way, you don't need to feel inferior to anyone who is already driving a car you want and living in a house you wish you had. Be patient. Don't worry; your time will come. Keep working!

Don't worry if you've not been paid yet. Some people are paid daily, some weekly, some monthly, and some yearly. You will soon be rewarded for your hard work.

Go for Gold

There are more people at the bottom and fewer people at the top because those at the bottom don't think there is space for them at the top. There is a place for you if you can see it and if you are ready to work to get it.

The sky is big enough for every bird to fly.

In life, everyone has the chance to get a gold medal. Why? We are all in our own individual races. Everyone should personally define what success means to them. What prize do you want to win at the end of your race? What does your gold medal represent? Remember: there is a price to pay for every prize. The bigger the prize, the bigger the price. The work required to get an A grade in school is greater than the work required to get a C grade. The work required to break the 100m sprint record is greater than the work required if you only want to be a participant in the race. It's your life, it's your race. You decide the prize (you set the goals), and you decide how fast you want to run to get it.

- Whether you get the prize or not is up to you. There is no one else to credit or to blame.
- There is no one else in your race to distract you. **The only person who can distract you is you**.

Lane 1: Me
Lane 2: Myself
Lane 3: I.

Pay careful attention to your own work, for then you will get the satisfaction of a job well done, and you won't need to compare yourself to anyone else. For we are each responsible for our own conduct.
Galatians 6:4

Don't Compare

Don't compare yourself with other people and use other people as a standard of measurement (2 Corinthians 10:12, paraphrased).

Consider this example: The runner says to the swimmer, "I am faster than you." The swimmer replied, "You are faster than me on the track, but you are not faster than me in the water. The track is your territory; the pool is mine." Don't copy others; you are a star in your own race!

Don't copy others; find out your own purpose.

Tim: Hey, Joe! God just gave me a revelation that I should open up my own coffee shop.

Joe: That is a great idea; this is a great environment for a coffee shop. There's none in the area. I'll open mine too.

Tim: Wait, Joe. It is a good idea but God told me, not you. Ask God for your own purpose.

Joe: Why? A good idea is always a good idea.

Tim: No. Not every good idea is God's plan for you. You need to be sure. Proverbs 14:12 says "There is a path before each person that seems right, but it ends in death."

Joe: (laughs) You don't want me to open my own coffee shop, so I won't take all your customers.

Tim: No, no, no! I want you to be sure of what you are going into.

Tim: When God told me to open my shop, he gave me a name for the shop, and he gave me all the details. I have the step-by-step action plan here and I feel a strong sense of urgency in me. This is my purpose for living. This is my calling.

Joe: Purpose? Can't I choose my purpose?

Tim: No, it doesn't work like that. God reveals your purpose to you; you don't just choose anything you want.

Tim: God is our manufacturer; we are his product, and he knows our purpose because he created us. It is our job to discover what it is.

Joe: How?

Tim: Ask God, "What am I created for? What is your purpose for me here on earth?"

Joe: After that, then what?

Tim: Wait and listen.

Joe: Ok.

Tim: Let's meet later this week to talk more.

Joe: Ok.

(They both go away. Joe asked God, but he didn't wait to hear from God. He couldn't take no for an answer. He was convinced that he wanted to open a coffee shop.)

(They met again during the week.)

Joe: Tim, I'm convinced, the coffee shop will work.

Tim: Ok.

(They both open their shops on opposite sides of the street. After two weeks, Tim had 500 regular customers a day; however, Joe had only five regular customers a day. Joe was struggling. He started to beg people to come into the shop, but they didn't come. Eventually he had to close down.)

Lessons learned:

- God knows your purpose; ask him and wait to hear his response.
- Don't copy others even if their businesses look attractive.
- You are a star in your own race. Don't settle for average in someone else's race.

Out of God's Purpose = Frustration

A person becomes very frustrated when they are doing something they were not created to do. Such a person will go around in circles.

Life becomes an endless struggle. For example, how difficult would it be to eat rice with a knife? How easy would it be to eat rice with a spoon? The purpose of a knife is cutting; when you try to use a knife for something else outside of its purpose, you will get frustrated.

With reference to the example above, using the knife again and again will not turn the knife into a spoon. The only way to use a spoon is to stop using the knife and pick up a spoon. Similarly, the only way you will ever discover your true purpose is to stop whatever you are doing and ask God for direction, so you can get back on track. You need to be humble and acknowledge that you made a mistake. Then, turn to the correct path. People may mock you, but it's your life, not theirs.

Final words to meditate on:

It doesn't matter how long you travel in the wrong direction, you will never get to your final destination.

"Your dominion is in your domain."
(Pastor Sunday Okomoda, Winners Chapel Connecticut)

Once you discover your reason for living, you will not envy any other person.

"Once you discover who you are, you will be free from everybody else's opinion."
(Dr. Myles Munroe)

We are all on the run; nobody wants to lose. The sooner you discover your race and start running, the better.

You are not too young to start walking in your purpose:

Josiah was eight years old when he became king, and he reigned in Jerusalem thirty-one years…He did what was pleasing in the Lord's sight and followed the example of his ancestor David. He did not turn away from doing what was right.
2 Kings 22: 1-2

Run to Win

Don't you realize that in a race everyone runs, but only one person gets the prize? So run to win! All athletes are disciplined in their training. They do it to win a prize that will fade away, but we do it for an eternal prize. So I run with purpose in every step. I am not just shadowboxing. I discipline my body like an athlete, training it to do what it should. Otherwise, I fear that after preaching to others I myself might be disqualified.
1 Corinthians 9:24-27

Let us follow Paul's example, he said,

I focus on this one thing: Forgetting the past and looking forward to what lies ahead, I press on to reach the end of the race and receive the heavenly prize for which God, through Christ Jesus, is calling us.
Philippians 4:13-14

The greatest joy we can all have is to say at the end of the race:

I have fought the good fight, I have finished the race, and I have remained faithful.
2 Timothy 4:7

HEART TO HEART

Bob: Let's say, I've just discovered my purpose or my race as you say. What time would you advise me to start running?

Ike: Start Now. Your time is now.

YOUR TIME IS NOW!

Live each day like it's your last.
Don't worry about the past;
Don't be mad-
Just be glad.
Live each day like it's your last.

The race of life is so real;
Please don't move like a seal.
Think well and move fast
So you don't end up finishing last.

There's a time to work
And a time to play.
Time waits for no one;
Let's make the most of today.

There are 24 hours in a day;
Some people use it, some abuse it, and some just throw it away.
Let us sit up and invest our time:
What we achieve now can feed us for a lifetime.

Need for Urgency

*We must quickly carry out the tasks assigned
us by the one who sent us. The night is
coming, and then no one can work.*
John 9:4

I like the way The Message Bible explains John 9:4:

*We need to be energetically at work for the One who
sent us here, working while the sun shines.
When night falls, the workday is over.*
John 9:4

We are not working for ourselves; we are working for God. God sent us to Planet Earth for a purpose. We must move with urgency, just like Noah. In Genesis, God told Noah about an unseen event (a flood), and Noah moved with godly fear and urgency. He built an ark and he saved his family (Hebrews 11:7, paraphrased). Let us move like Noah. (For the full story, read from Genesis chapter 6).

Pay Now or Pay Later

If we don't work hard now, we will be working harder tomorrow under those who have worked hard today. Everybody wants to enjoy old age. Nobody wants to be stressing themselves when they are old, but we have to work now, so we can enjoy the fruits of our labor later.

*Lazy people are soon poor; hard workers get rich. A
wise youth works hard all summer; a youth who sleeps
away the hour of opportunity brings shame.*
Proverbs 10:4-5

Don't Be Lazy: What You Sow, You Will Reap.

Plant Nothing; Harvest Nothing!

Peter: John, come along; this is planting season, and we must plant as many seeds as possible so we can gather a huge harvest when it comes.

John: No, I'm okay. I need to sleep. You guys are working too hard; take it easy. Relax.

Peter: John, remember what Proverbs 10: 5 says? "A wise youth works hard all summer; a youth who sleeps away the hour of opportunity brings shame."

John: Okay. (John starts snoring.)

(Harvest time! Peter and James go to the farm. John follows them with a big smile on his face, expecting a harvest. Peter and James start to pick the corn they had planted, and John starts to pick the corn too.)

Peter: John, what are you doing?

John: I am picking the corn I planted.

Peter: You didn't plant any corn.

John: What do you mean I didn't plant any corn? We always plant together.

James: (with disappointment) Not this time. You didn't join us when we came to plant.

Peter: I asked you to come and you were sleeping. Also, you said, "you guys are working too hard; take it easy. Relax."

James: We sowed corn seeds, and now it's time for us to reap corn. You sowed nothing, so you reap nothing. Sorry, John.

...for whatever a man sows is what he will reap.
Galatians 6:7 (Amplified Bible).

- Work today, so you can rest tomorrow; if you sleep too much today, you may be a beggar tomorrow.
- Time waits for nobody. You can choose to run ahead of time, to run behind time, to run with time, or to waste time. One thing is for sure, time keeps moving. You decide how you use your time.

HEART TO HEART

Ike: Bob, it's been a great journey.

Bob: Oh yes. I've learned a lot.

Ike: We are still friends, but we need to separate for a while.

Bob: Why?

Ike: So we can focus and apply these principles to our lives. In four years from now, we can go to lunch to discuss our progress.

Bob: Who's paying?

Ike: It won't matter because we'll both be successful, if we work hard now. My future is my responsibility; your future is your responsibility.

MY FUTURE IS MY RESPONSIBILITY

If I want to go up, there are some things I have to give up.
If I want the A, there is a price I have to pay.
If I want to go to new heights, I have to get on board the flight.
If I must go higher, sometimes I have to go through the fire.
If I want to move fast, I have to let go of the past.
If I want to fulfill my calling, I cannot be afraid of falling.
If I want to do the impossible, I am responsible.
If I want results, I cannot be moved by insults.
If I want to see the light, I have to endure the fright.
If I must taste the better, sometimes I have to bite through the bitter.
If I don't want to end up a thief, I have to roll up my sleeve.
If I don't want to be poor, I must keep knocking at every door.
If I want to get hired, I must not get tired.
If I want fresh fish, I can't sit down and make a wish.
If I want to move to new levels, I need to defeat the old devils.
If I don't want to change diapers now, I can't get too hyper.
If I don't want to be outdated, I need to get myself updated.
If I want to be ahead, I need to read instead.
If I must see the gains, I have to endure the pains.
If I want to be an attraction, I need to avoid distraction.
If I want a good year, I have to overcome my fear.

Heart to Heart

Bob: Why does every line start with *if*?
Ike: It's because every good thing you want in your life is a choice.
If you want it, you can have it *if* you take responsibility.

My formula for success

Faith + Hard Work = Success (when you are successful, some people may say you are lucky because they've seen the results, but they haven't seen the work.) Faith is work. Hard Work is work. There's nothing lucky about the equation. Success is deliberately and consciously pursued. There is no substitute for hard work. **So don't wish your neighbor "good luck," wish them "good work."**

A wise man said, "I'm not lucky, I'm worky."

You are pregnant with greatness-push it out.

Everything you need to be successful is inside you already. You have the potential. Just like a baby is inside a pregnant woman-greatness is inside you. But, that baby will only come out and be in her hands if she pushes. In the same way, your greatness will only be a reality if you push it out. No shortcuts or C-sections.

Good planning and hard work lead to prosperity,
but hasty shortcuts lead to poverty.
Proverbs 21:5

The reason why some people work hard but don't get the full rewards for their labor is because they stop before the finish line. They get off to a good start, they take big strides, but they give up.

It's time to push that idea, business, career, book, or invention out of you.

CONCLUSION

Tomorrow may be too late

· · · · · · · · · · ●· · · · · · · · · · · ·

I've got time
Tomorrow will always come
If I don't do it today
Tomorrow it will be done.

Tomorrow didn't come
He arrived today, Judgement day is today.
Now you face the judge
Before him, all actions are weighed

· · · · · · · · · · ●· · · · · · · · · · · ·

12 "Look, I am coming soon, bringing my reward with me to repay all people according to their deeds.
13 I am the Alpha and the Omega, the First and the Last, the Beginning and the End."
14 Blessed are those who wash their robes. They will be permitted to enter through the gates of the city and eat the fruit from the tree of life.

Revelation 22:12-14

Salvation is the key

Salvation is the key to unlock all the blessings from the truths outlined in this book. Many people know about God, but they don't have a relationship with God. God is not looking for religious people;

God wants a relationship with you. The life of a Christian is filled with blessings, favour, wonders, and great miracles. I am a living proof. This book is a living proof. I can't take any credit. I wrote this book by the inspiration of God. I downloaded from Heaven and I uploaded my results unto the pages of this book. I can boldly declare any day and anytime: ***God is real and God is good.*** It is something to be experienced, not just explained. I pray that you will experience God for yourself. You may doubt what someone tells you but you can't doubt what you have seen for yourself.

Are you in or out?

I was born into a Christian family, I went to church, I was even an usher in church but I knew that I wasn't fully walking with God. I was a religious person, but I was not in a relationship with God. I wanted the fun that comes with worldly living and the blessings that come with Godly living, but this is not how it works. I was standing on the fence, also known as being lukewarm (not hot or cold, not too good and not too bad). Well, here is what the Bible says about this:

> *I know all the things you do, that you*
> *are neither hot nor cold.*
> *I wish that you were one or the other! But since*
> *you are like lukewarm water, neither hot nor*
> *cold, I will spit you out of my mouth!*
> **Revelation 3:15-16**

Make sure

If you are not saved, everything else we've discussed won't work, because the key component, the Greatest component is missing-God. Without God, nothing will work. Without God, we can forget about excellence, safety, favour, etc. These are all benefits that come with having a relationship with God. You may have given your life to Jesus before but you don't remember the date or the place. Please, do it again to make sure. Salvation is something we must do personally. There is no such thing as group salvation; we must all individually confess Jesus as our Lord and Saviour. We must carry our cross individually.

If any of you wants to be my follower, you must turn from your selfish ways, take up your cross daily, and follow me
Luke 9: 23

No one can eat for you. You cannot say after you are born, "Mum, I am hungry, please eat for me." In the same way, no one can step out to accept salvation for you. Our parent's salvation can't cover ours. As my Mum always says to us with love and sincerity, "You are born already. I have my life to live; you have your life to live." Good parents are direct. They don't try and sugarcoat these issues. God will hold them responsible if they are not sincere with their children. There is life after death and we will all be accountable for our actions individually. So don't let anyone deceive you.

The decision that changed my life

I have given my life to Christ on many occasions before without proper understanding. However, on one blessed day, June 10, 2012, I gave my life to Christ and I wrote the date down this time. I was baptized in water by immersion on December 30, 2012, and my life has never remained the same.

Please say this prayer if you haven't already:

"Father, I know that I have broken your laws and my sins have separated me from you. I am truly sorry, and now I want to turn away from my past sinful life toward you. Please forgive me, and help me avoid sinning again. I believe that your son, Jesus Christ died for my sins, was resurrected from the dead, is alive, and hears my prayer. I invite Jesus to become the Lord of my life, to rule and reign in my heart from this day forward. Please send your Holy Spirit to help me obey You, and to do Your will for the rest of my life. In Jesus' name I pray, Amen." (Source: www.allaboutgod.com)

Congratulations, if you have prayed this prayer from your heart, you are now saved. Find a local church, where you can be baptized and continue to grow in the knowledge of God through his Word, the Bible. You've made a decision that you will never regret forever. I look forward to seeing and hearing your testimonies.

Closing Message:

I hope you were empowered by this book and you will apply what you have learned to your life. I pray that this book will be a lifetime blessing to you and whoever you decide to share it with. Although this book was written by me, the book is also for me. Every word and every instruction applies to me too. As I'm educating and motivating others to make progress, I'm also striving to make progress daily.

If you have any questions regarding anything I talked about in this book, contact me. If you desire mentoring, feel free to contact me. I am also available to speak on any of the topics outlined in this book. Feel free to contact me to discuss your needs or the needs of your audience.

It's your time to Shine! God bless you.

Website	: www.ikeekwueme.com	Twitter	: @IkeEkwueme
Email	: ekwueme.ike@gmail.com	YouTube	: Ike Ekwueme
Facebook	: Ike Ekwueme	Skype	: ike.ekwueme

There is a growing need for positive role models who understand the importance of investing their energy, their time and their hearts toward their goals. Ike Ekwueme, Valedictorian, and 4.0 GPA college graduate, was not always so dedicated. In high school, he made a decision to develop himself spiritually and physically which led to a significant turnaround in his life. This season of self-development was not a waste as it opened the door for an academic and soccer scholarship in America. Today he is spreading his message of hope, tenacity, and possibility to students across the world who are in need of an inspiring role model. His unique global perspective makes him the perfect speaker to encourage, enlighten, and motivate students toward the path of excellence.

IKE IS A DYNAMIC SPEAKER WHO COVERS A WIDE RANGE OF SPIRITUAL AND MOTIVATIONAL TOPICS.

"Motivating the youth to take personal responsibility for their lives, realize the joy of hard work and graduate with a sense of fulfillment!"

—Ike Ekwueme

Email: ekwueme.ike@gmail.com | Website: www.ikeekwueme.com

Note from the Publisher

Are you a first time author?

Not sure how to proceed to get your book published?
Want to keep all your rights and all your royalties?
Want it to look as good as a Top 10 publisher?
Need help with editing, layout, cover design?
Want it out there selling in 90 days or less?

Visit our website for some exciting new options!

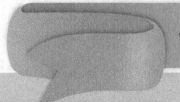

www.chalfant-eckert-publishing.com

Lightning Source UK Ltd.
Milton Keynes UK
UKOW06f2342021115

261947UK00001B/29/P